My Dog Thinks He's Human

50 Ways to a Happy Healthy Pet

My Dog Thinks He's Human

50 Ways to a Happy Healthy Pet

Peter Wedderburn

Illustrated by Per José Karlén

spruce

An Hachette UK Company
First published in Great Britain in 2009 by Spruce
a division of Octopus Publishing Group Ltd
2–4 Heron Quays, London E14 4JP.
www.octopusbooks.co.uk
www.octopusbooksusa.com

Distributed in the U.S. and Canada for Octopus Books USA
Hachette Book Group USA
237 Park Avenue
New York NY 10017.

ISBN 13 978-1-84601-339-3
ISBN 10 1-84601-339-9

A CIP catalogue record for this book is available from the
British Library.

Printed and bound in China
10 9 8 7 6 5 4 3 2 1

The advice given here should not be used as a
substitute for that of a veterinary surgeon. The reader
should consult a veterinary surgeon in all matters
relating to the health of the dog. While the advice
and information are believed to be accurate
and true at the time of going to press, neither
the author nor the publisher can accept legal
responsibility or liability for any errors or
omissions that my have been made.

CONTENTS

Introduction 8

A DOG'S DINNER 10

How can I be sure that his diet is balanced?

Posh nosh or basic rations?

When it comes to dining, watch out for the small print.

Delicious treats or toxic truffles?

A butchers' bone – can it harm him?

Does eating grass mean he's vegetarian?

My dog has a gassy problem. What can I do about it?

The vet says he is fat, but I think he looks cute. Who's right?

He barks at me for a cup of tea. Is it OK to give him some?

FROM MANGY MUTT TO PAMPERED POOCH 24

How can I make sure his friends don't share their
fleas with him, too?

Don't let your dog give grooming the brush off.

He drenches the house after his baths. Will a bathrobe help?

My dog is moulting. Is he likely to go bald?

Why does he refuse to wear the lovely jacket I bought him?

It is nail-biting stuff! Why won't he let me clip his nails?

Silver threads amongst the gold. Can you get hair dye for dogs?

His teeth have gone brown. Should I start brushing them?

CANINE CRIMES 36

How can I teach him not to bite when we're playing?

How can I get him to tone down his hysteria when I get home?

To pee or not to pee?

When is a bed not a bed?

What can I do to ensure my new dog doesn't turn out neurotic?

Should I be feeding my dog from my plate?

Is it true that there are high chairs for dogs?

Why does he do what he wants, not what I tell him to do?

Why does he sledge his bottom along the ground?

How can I persuade him that a simple handshake is enough?

Why does my dog love chasing things?

A WALK IN THE PARK 52

Just who's walking whom?

He often looks sad. How can I cheer him up?

He's such a lazy dog. What can I do?

Why doesn't he come back when I call him?

How can I teach him that rolling in horse manure
is simply not good?

Where's the stop button?

How can I stop him barking in the car?

DOG GONE! 62

Should I encourage my dog to be a bit more independent?

My garden is becoming as tunnel infested as the Great Escape!

He loves his own voice, but it is driving us mad!

How can I stop him escaping from the garden?

How can we make sure he has a good time when we're away?

Dog Day Afternoon...TV matinees for mutts?

SICK AS A DOG? 72

Should I introduce him to puppy love?

How can I make him be more pleasant to his doctor?

Walking when he hasn't had his puppy shots.
Is it worth the risk?

Should I stop my dog licking my face?

How often should his bedding be changed?

Doggy breath?

To insure or not to insure?

He always refuses to take his tablets. Any tips?

Will my dog forgive me for having him neutered?

Author biography 84

Introduction

Dogs share our homes and our lives in a closer
way than any other pet. A dog becomes as much
a member of the family as any member of the
household, included in photographs and storytelling.
Humans often treat their dogs like little humans,
and so it's no wonder that they behave as if they
are one. But dogs are just that...dogs! And to be
happy pets, they need to be treated like dogs, so
that they think they are dogs.

8

This doesn't mean you need to be a tough disciplinarian at all times, nor do you need to whisper quiet messages into your dog's ears. But you do need to be Top Dog, and you need to discover that sometimes the best way to treat your dog is different to what you may feel like doing. There are times for spoiling dogs and times for being more assertive. Every dog is different and while there are no universal rules, it is possible to have broad guidelines that apply to every dog and owner. That's what this book is about. It includes 50 suggestions for looking after your dog in the best possible way, including tips on health and training.

Life together should be a pleasure – for human and dog. The aim of this book is to help you both enjoy your relationship to the full.

CHAPTER 1

a dog's dinner

How can I be sure that his diet is balanced?

His choices are:
1. Moist dog food with dog 'mixer' biscuits.
2. Dried 'complete' food.
3. Home-cooked meals.

Your vet will tell you what he thinks is good for him and Fido will tell you what he thinks is tasty! If you put down what's good for him and he eats it, he'll be happy and healthy. If he chooses not to eat it, tweak the ingredients a bit, but stay this side of the 'what's-good-for-him' fence and soon you'll strike the right balance. This may be a mix of moist food and mixer biscuits or a dried 'complete' food designed specially for dogs, but don't forget the fresh water beside his food bowl. Don't stuff him on cakes, curries and spaghetti Bolognese, and do remember that Fido, like you, has discerning taste buds. It's OK to spoil him from time to time. Occasional portions of delicately seasoned fish and vegetables or a slice of roast beef with gravy will be enthusiastically received.

Posh nosh or basic rations?

Commercial dog food varies as much in quality as it does in price. You can take the nutritionist's word on this or you can try a simple experiment at home for yourself. Feed your dog a high-quality diet for two months and judge the difference for yourself.

Rule of thumb: dogs that are fed on quality foods tend to look bright-eyed and bushy-tailed, while those fed on a cheaper diet, which consists of a high percentage of indigestible bulking agents, not only look less healthy but also require a correspondingly higher percentage of poop-scooping!

When it comes to dining, watch out for the small print.

Your dog is what you feed him, so if he's hyperactive and uncontrollable, check his diet. Avoid the foods that have a bewildering list of additives and derivatives, and choose brands with ingredients that you can understand. You wouldn't give a child a handful of candy containing tartrazine after it has been proven that it causes hyperactivity in children. Your pooch is just as sensitive.

Delicious treats or toxic truffles?

The stimulants in chocolate are highly poisonous and potentially fatal to dogs, causing their heart to beat too rapidly. The toxic dose depends on the weight of the dog, so that smaller dogs are most vulnerable. Whilst dark chocolate is better for us, it is three times more toxic than milk chocolate for dogs, and as little as 25g (1oz) could be enough to kill a 3kg (6½-lb) Yorkshire terrier. Store all chocolate out of dog-reach – most fatalities happen when dogs consume entire boxes of chocolates that have been accidentally left within grabbing distance.

You may feel guilty looking into those big sad eyes, but you may just be saving Fido's life by saying No. Find another type of treat that is safe for him. Chopped-up cooked sausages or dried liver treats may not appeal to you, but your dog will adore them.

A butchers' bone — can it harm him?

Yes. The sharp pieces of a raw bone can get lodged in his digestive tract, causing an obstruction that requires complex surgery to resolve. In addition, the small fragments of bone can accumulate and solidify in the lower bowel, forming a concrete-like block that can be very difficult to remove. It's safer to give him manufactured nutritional chews, or a chew toy such as a Kong, stuffed with food. If you really want to give him bones, buy some pre-cooked beef shins and knuckles from the pet shop. These are less likely to splinter, and won't carry the risk of a bacterial infection that could be passed on from raw bones.

Does eating grass mean he's vegetarian?

Dogs are omnivorous, enjoying both meat and vegetable components in their diet. And most do enjoy occasional grazing on grass, picking out leafy stems and chewing contentedly. Nobody knows exactly why dogs do this; perhaps for additional nutrients that may be missing from their diet? Some dogs vomit after eating grass, suggesting that they deliberately make themselves sick if they are feeling a little nauseous. There is probably no single answer, and every dog may chew grass for a different reason. It's nothing to worry about, as long as the grass is free of pesticides and it causes no other physical problems.

My dog has a gassy problem. What can I do about it?

Nobody enjoys the company of a flatulent dog. If pooch has a gassy problem, look at his protein consumption. Introduce him to a specifically designed 'highly digestible', dry biscuit diet, available from your vet or pet shop. Feed him smaller portions more often. Alternatively, try a different meat source, such as duck, fish or venison sold as special single-protein diets available through vets. If these changes don't clear the air, then either visit your vet or invest in some gas masks.

The vet says he is fat, but I think he looks cute. Who's right?

If the vet says your dog is overweight then he IS, no matter how hard you try to convince yourself that he is merely 'well covered', and at five years old, it isn't puppy fat any longer. The loving solution is to put porky pooch on a diet and not be tempted to give unnecessary treats. Research some light diets online to find one that has the right nutritional balance for your dog, then stick to it. The most effective low-calorie diets are kept as 'prescription-only' products, supplied by vets for those patients that really need them. Many vets have free obesity clinics with regular weigh-ins so that you can track pooch's progress back to healthy happiness.

He barks at me for a cup of tea. Is it OK to give him some?

No! Caffeine in tea and coffee can be toxic to dogs. A 284ml (half-pint) cup of tea contains around 60mg of caffeine, instant coffee up to 100mg, and the real stuff a colossal 175mg. A skinny latte may be fairly safe for a large Labrador, but half a cup of tea could be enough to cause serious problems for a toy poodle. He may bark for a cuppa, but if you ignore his commands, he'll soon get the message.

CHAPTER 2

from mangy mutt to pampered pooch

How can I make sure his friends don't share their fleas with him, too?

The long and the short of it is that fleas jump from dog to dog regardless of who owns them. Whether your corgi is of royal stock or a tearaway, you should use a once-monthly vial of flea drops, which is applied to the skin between his shoulder blades. This leaves a continual presence of anti-flea substance in his skin or bloodstream, so that if a flea lands on him, it will not survive for long. Ask your vet about the best version of drops available and suggested usage. If your dog does get fleas, you will also need to treat for tapeworms, which are transmitted by dogs swallowing the fleas that they nibble out of their own coats. And remember, the rich itch too!

Don't let your dog give grooming the brush off.

From a dog's perspective, it's easy to see why grooming may look like a game. You come towards him, holding a 'toy' in your hand (he doesn't know it's a brush). You wave it around, and when he tries to grab it, you wave it even more. To him, it looks like the stuff you do in the park. You need to combine basic dog training with gentle grooming. Teach him to sit and stay on command, and keep rewarding him (with praise and treats) as long as he remains sitting still. When he can do this, take out the brush, and do some simple grooming, continuing to reward him for behaving well. Do a little bit each day and in no time Mr Scruff will be looking like Mr Sleek.

He drenches the house after his baths. Will a bathrobe help?

Luxury warm and snug bathrobes are available for dogs but manufacturers warn that they are a fashion accessories and should be worn only under supervision. A better way to avoid saturating the house is to plan 'bath day' more carefully. The options are:

1. On a fine day, wash outside, where he can race around drying *au naturel*.
2. Limit the affair to just one room and line it with newspaper.
3. Place an extra-large, high-absorption towel in his bed. Towel dry him as best you can, then entice him into his bed, with some attention-grabbing device to keep him occupied.
4. Give up. Use a professional groomer.

My dog is moulting. Is he likely to go bald?

You can put away that hair-restorer because it's normal for dogs to shed fur in small quantities all year round. Once or twice a year also, most dogs have a heavy moult. In the spring, the long, dense winter coat is replaced by a lighter summer coat, with the process happening again in reverse in the autumn. Despite this normal hair loss, it's unlikely your dog will ever have bald patches.

Frequent grooming is the best way to prevent moulting hair getting onto your carpets and furniture. Other ways to remove hair include taking your dog for walks in dense undergrowth and giving him a bath and towelling him dry thoroughly. And if you have an exceptionally laid-back pooch, try the vacuum cleaner.

Why does he refuse to wear the lovely jacket I bought him?

Do you blame him? Dogs only wear clothes because their owners make them. Forcing a dog to wear clothes when he doesn't want to is tantamount to cruelty.

That said, there are several scenarios when clothing for dogs can be useful: for example, if a long-haired dog has been clipped short, he can get cold and might appreciate an extra layer. Fine-haired or very small dogs might be glad of protection from heavy rain, a dog with an allergy to grass may enjoy a protective layer and a dog who for medical reasons has lost large patches of his coat can be misconceived as having been mistreated by its owner, so a light cover might avoid confused protests and embarrassments in the street. Otherwise, go with what nature intended, and if anyone must be forced to wear a tartan vest and booties with pom-poms, better that it is you!

It is nail-biting stuff!
Why won't he let me clip his nails?

The closest thing I have encountered to a Great White Shark is a Welsh terrier who didn't like having his nails trimmed! Dogs are drama queens and just the mention of nails can send them into absolute fits of distress, howling and growling. And rightly so: if you cut too much nail, you could end up nicking the quick, causing pain and bleeding.

Start gradually when he is still a puppy and take the process a bit further each time, first by physically restraining him and rewarding him as long as he stays calm and relaxed. Next time, pick up one foot, and examine it, then each foot in detail. If he lets you do this without a fuss, move on to clipping the sharp tip of one nail. Remember to reward and praise all along. Do two nails the following day and so forth. If he starts to struggle, go back a step. Any lack of confidence on your part is quickly telegraphed to your dog, and remember, a dog has teeth!

Silver threads amongst the gold. Can you get hair dye for dogs?

Here we go again! Can't a dog age in peace without human vanity getting in the way? For heavens sake, dogs age too and a salt-and-pepper coat can look distinguished. Besides, one should be asking what can be done to extend his life and make his old age comfortable, not how to cover it up. Many older dogs begin to suffer from perfectly treatable problems that are not recognized by their owners, including arthritis and dental disease. Speak to your vet, who may suggest a special diet designed for older dogs that may help to optimize his physical state, mental health and appearance in his later years, and save the blue rinse for yourself.

His teeth have gone brown. Should I start brushing them?

To optimize dental health, all dogs should have their teeth brushed on a regular basis from puppyhood onwards. The question is this: do you really want to get into your dog's mouth? Most people accept the trade-off: they don't brush their dog's teeth, and their pets develop moderate dental disease as they get older. If your pet has got to the stage where he has significant build-up of tartar, you will need to ask the vet to clean up his teeth under anaesthesia. If you do choose to brush his teeth and give him that Hollywood smile, ask your vet about the best toothbrush and toothpaste to use. Anyone for raw chicken-seasoned toothpaste?

CHAPTER 3

canine crimes

How can I teach him not to bite when we're playing?

Puppies learn 'bite inhibition' between the ages of 2 and 12 weeks from their siblings, but since they go to new homes at around 8 weeks, it is up to new owners to complete the life lessons about how hard to bite without causing harm. No, I am not asking you to bite your puppy. But if he bites you, you should say 'ouch' loudly, and withdraw your attention. If he does it again, say it more loudly, and leave the room until he learns that certain biting results in adverse consequences and stops doing it. As he grows, teach him in a similar fashion not to grab people, however gently. Provided you remain in control, there is nothing wrong with a little rough and tumble, but if things do get out of control, step back and consider whether you are teaching him the right lessons. If not, get help from a professional dog trainer to put his development back on track.

How can I get him to tone down his hysteria when I get home?

This is a common problem and easy to fix. You have accidentally trained your dog to be like this. When you come home, and he gives you lots of adoring attention, you respond by greeting him enthusiastically in return, rewarding him for behaving in that way.

To re-train him, you have to behave in a way that seems intuitively wrong if not cruel: you ignore him completely when you get home, and act as if he isn't there. Just do your own business while blanking him completely. When he doesn't get a response from you, he will eventually settle down. Once he has calmed down, you can then call him over to you, and greet him as he has never been greeted before. If you adhere to this new routine for a few weeks, you will find that he becomes a much-composed beastie.

To pee or not to pee?

None of us likes to come downstairs half asleep, barefooted, only to be shocked into the new day by stepping in something wet and stinky on the floor. Shocked as you may be, rubbing his nose in his mishaps or shouting at him is counterproductive.
It takes about 14 weeks for a puppy to be house trained, so until then use your own radar to seek out the tell-tale signs of when he is likely to need to go. When he wakes, soon after eating, when he seems restless or begins that peculiar, directionless circling walk dogs do with head down and tail up, get him outdoors. When he does get it right, make a fuss and reward him. You'll soon be back to being barefoot with confidence.

When is a bed not a bed?

So, your dog has taken over your sofa! Well what are you going to do about it? Be a pussycat and let him take control? Get back to being leader of the pack, reclaim what is rightfully yours and show him where his own bed is. From pooch's perspective it is probably down to you that he is there in the first place. Something you have done has made him feel it is OK for him to be there. Now you have to break the habit and create a new rule…and stick to it. Make the sofa less appealing to him than his own bed…place some treats in his bed, reward him when he goes and settles there and perhaps plug-in a DAP diffuser to spray soothing pheromones into the air beside him. Soon he will be comfortable knowing his place and you can be king of the castle again.

What can I do to ensure my new dog doesn't turn out neurotic?

In the first place, choose a dog with the genes of a calm dog! If you are getting a puppy, try to arrange to meet both parents to see if they are obedient, relaxed dogs. If they are, then there is a strong possibility your puppy will turn out the same way. If they are bloodthirsty, salivating beasts with a killer glint in their eye and a growl to match, avoid their puppy for the same reasons!

Don't select the nervous shivering mutt in the corner just because his big, sad eyes make you want to hug him! After all, what you are looking for is an emotionally stable, cheerful and contented dog. Any signs to the contrary should be taken as warning bells unless you are a skilled dog trainer or canine psychiatrist.

Are you, as his owner, as well balanced as the dog you seek? Or are you a little over-anxious, over-sensitive and obsessive? With regular obedience training, socializing, routine walks and, if necessary, a good dog trainer, owners and their dogs become as well adjusted and well behaved as each other.

Should I be feeding my dog from my plate?

When it comes to mealtimes it pays to remember just who is Top Dog! Feed your dog from your plate and soon he'll expect you to set a place at the dinner table…and the breakfast bar too! Your dog will gladly chow down on anything he's offered, so it is your responsibility to give him the balanced diet he needs to stay healthy, otherwise the person to blame when he's grown too fat to groom his extremities will be YOU! Weigh him regularly and use common sense. If you already have a chubby salivating canine hovering by the table, place him in another room at mealtimes.

Is it true that there are high chairs for dogs?

It is possible to buy a high chair specially designed for dogs, complete with a lead clip so he doesn't irresponsibly clamber out of the chair and all over your elegant table arrangement. But it is probably smarter to recognize that he is a dog and happy dogs should learn to sit quietly wherever is appropriate during dinner. They may appear to thrive on pampering but it is vital to have clear lines that separate the species. A dog sitting at the table for dinner has clearly strayed into human territory.

Why does he do what he wants, not what I tell him to do?

It's no good trying to reason with your pet as though he were human. Dogs need to be told and to learn to do what they are told. A successful owner–dog relationship depends upon you being in control and teaching him appropriate boundaries. If a dog does what he wants in small, harmless ways, it is likely that he may start to do what he wants in big, annoying, even dangerous ways. Before you know it, he will growl when he doesn't get his way, possibly biting people who try to interfere. If you are not confident about retraining your canine lout into a happy socialized dog, seek professional help. Otherwise, prepare to get snarled at!

Why does he sledge his bottom along the ground?

Suddenly your dog seems to have learned a strange new trick. He places his bottom on the floor and drags himself along as though riding on a sledge. It is possible that he has worked out that this activity gets extra attention from you, even if that attention involves you being annoyed with him. The message is simple: don't let him annoy you, because this will only make the problem worse.

The bottom sledging is not a new trick at all, but probably one of three things. Firstly, anal glands can become clogged and sometimes infected: your vet may need to attend to these. Secondly, some worms can cause itchiness beneath the tail, so give a broad-spectrum worm dose at least once every three months. And finally, there is a long list of skin diseases that can cause localized itchiness: again, this is one to work through with your vet. Pooch doesn't mean to entertain you or to annoy you...he's just got an itch!

How can I persuade him that a simple handshake is enough?

If you were a dog and the doorbell started ringing, then new faces and voices appeared and a level of heightened excitement suddenly took grip on the house, I suspect you would bark and jump up on visitors, too. What is needed here is some basic training. If you spent 15 minutes daily working with your dog to stay on all four feet, even when excited, you could change his bad habits over weeks and months. The quick fix is to automatically put your dog away when visitors arrive. Once everyone has calmed down, then let him come in. He'll be much less likely to jump up in the same way. Once you have him trained not to jump up any more, you can begin to work on his handshake.

Why does my dog love chasing things?

Dogs are dogs and that means they love chasing. Give them a chance and they'll chase anything that moves, from cats to skateboarders; joggers to double-decker buses. It stems from their ancestry as hunting or herding animals.

Chasing comes with its own reward, if you think about it. The dog barks and chases something and it goes away...so in effect he's won! The fact that it was just passing by anyway is neither here nor there. If it's a cat he is chasing and the cat turns and has a go at his nose with her claws, it may stop him chasing cats. If cyclists or joggers are your concern, ask one or several of them to come by and surprise him by giving an equivalent biff on the nose with a blast from a water pistol or loudly shaking a plastic bottle with pebbles in it. This may put him off the idea in future before there is some kind of accident.

But it is you who needs to be in control when there are such concerns around. Get him to walk in a controlled way beside you, remaining focused on you at all times so that even cyclists whizzing by are not enough to distract him. Reward him with praise or treats when he has behaved well.

CHAPTER 4

a walk in the park

Just who's walking whom?

Try to take this on board straight away. Your dog is a dog, not a little human! He has been bred from generations of other dogs to work alongside humans and will be happiest when he is obedient. If you obey him, then every time he wants to walk he will bark until he gets his way...and so it goes with everything. It will drive you barking mad! So ignore him, never concede. You choose the time and place. You be 'in charge' on walks. If he is unruly, use a Halti type of head collar or a no-pull body harness to control him. Enrol for dog-training classes, which will teach you both how to deal with issues like Sit...Come...Stay... Walk-at-Heel. Once the two of you have mastered these essential tasks, you should repeat the exercise daily, putting him through his paces, reminding him of his training and rewarding him when he successfully completes a command. Remember, life is like a dogsled team. If you aren't the lead dog, the scenery will never change.

He often looks sad.
How can I cheer him up?

Dogs are social creatures and are happiest when in contact with others, so, yes, the more time you spend with your dog the happier he will be. But that doesn't mean that when you are not with your dog he is unhappy. After a play or long walk with you, they will be perfectly happy to rest alone or groom themselves. Don't be fooled by their long or sad hangdog expressions. Many dog's facial expressions have been bred into them, so that Bassett Hounds or some Labradors will look sad even if you hand them a dish of cooked sausages!

He's such a lazy dog.
What can I do?

Dogs are rarely lazy in the same way as a human, but if the exercise is boring, dogs are as likely as humans to refuse to do it. Find a way to make exercise fun. This could involve giving him regular treats during a walk on a lead, changing the route of your normal walk so that he has a new battery of smells to get excited over, or it could mean sessions of chasing a tennis ball, or just plenty of attention from you when you are out together. Find out what reward motivates your dog, and then include some of that reward for him in your daily exercise regime to encourage him to be more active.

Why doesn't he come back when I call him.

Place yourself in your dog's position. You are running free and having a great time and someone calls you back...you go and they put you on your lead and stop all your fun. What does it teach you? Probably that there is no incentive to come back when called next time! Always have a reward ready for your dog when he comes back to you, and give him plenty of praise and attention. Do repeated recalls in training situations set up to be challenging, with other dogs and people around. Have food treats at hand to distract him or reward him even when he has learned to come back each time, so that he continues to associate coming back with a positive outcome.

How can I teach him that rolling in horse manure is simply not good?

Some people can't bear the smell of certain smells while others adore them. Some wear one scent to suggest one thing and on another occasion something subtler to communicate something else. It is just possible that the aroma of cow pats, fox pee or dead pheasant entrances your dog...so he rolls in it, wishing to carry that scent with him.

Of course, it may hark back to ancient instincts when it was used as a way of carrying a message back to the pack that a certain animal is in the vicinity, or it may be used as a disguise when going to hunt the creature that deposited it.

Whatever your dog's reason for rolling in muck, the best tactic is to pre-empt it. Call him to heel or keep him on a lead until you have passed the problem. But from now on, go easy on the aftershave or perfume yourself. He may simply wish to smell as unpleasant to you as you do to him.

Where's the stop button?

Your energy will never match your dog's energy. A crafty dog walker will come armed with a nifty device designed to add to the dog's exercise with minimal exertion by the handler. An excellent example of such a device is a toughened tennis ball with a long-handled launcher that sends the ball flying into the far distance to be retrieved by your pet while you continue at your own pace. Vary the exercise with the different devices available from good pet stores, such as a Kong on a rope or a floating version, to encourage your dog to swim. Dog Frisbees also fly long distances, giving your dog the workout he requires and you the relaxing stroll you deserve.

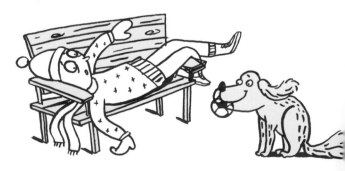

How can I stop him barking in the car?

Dogs feel very strongly that they should always go in the car with you, just in case the need should arise for them to bark in your ear! You probably brought it upon yourself by reacting to his *singing*, and he now thinks it's something you like. Some dogs get excited about travelling in the car; others get anxious. Ignore their noise and give them no reason to feel praised for doing it.

Begin his in-car training as a pup. If you have an adult dog that is excited in the car, you need to go back to basics. Start outside the car: training him to sit and stay. Keep him focused on you, as he sits still. Gradually move him towards the car, always rewarding him for being calm and relaxed. Put him in the car, then start the engine. The process should be done very slowly, not moving to the next step until the dog has succeeded in remaining relaxed.

CHAPTER 5

dog gone!

Should I encourage my dog to be a bit more independent?

Dogs enjoy company, but they need to be encouraged to enjoy being on their own, too. If you have a dog that trails beside you, always under your feet, you need to take action, for the dog's sake. Make sure his bed is not right beside your bed at night. When you go for walks, use a long lead to encourage him to explore the world a bit further away from you. Share the dog care, so that he doesn't see you as *the only one*. Encourage him with rewards to settle down a small distance from yourself by placing objects between the two of you (such as chairs or big cushions). Create a secure, homey environment for him when you are not there. Leave the radio on or consider using a DAP diffuser beside his bed, sending soothing dog pheromones into the air around him. Lastly, reward him with a special treat before you leave, and soon you'll find that he is encouraging you out of the door.

My garden is becoming as tunnel infested as the Great Escape!

One of the hardest things for an owner to do is stop their dog from doing something they really enjoy. Dogs love to dig holes. It is instinctive and harks back to their ancestor activities: making dens, looking for food or creating a cool spot in hot weather. Modern pet dogs dig for the simple reason that they enjoy it. Try to get him to learn where he can and cannot dig. Use a sand pit or soft earth bank where you can bury things for him to dig up, so he learns to dig on command and not through boredom, and reward him when he behaves well. If you leave him alone in the garden, leave him with something to do instead of digging while you are away.

He loves his own voice, but it is driving us mad!

When dogs get bored or want some human interaction, they bark, and barking has no volume control. To avoid a community meltdown, you need to do something about it now. Ensure that pooch has plenty of energy-depleting activities. Take him for a half-hour walk twice a day. Occupy his mind when he is outside by himself with a frozen food-stuffed Kong, or a food-releasing puzzle cube dog toy, taking care to decrease the amount of food you give him at his normal mealtime to ensure that he has enough of an appetite to be interested in these food-rewarding toys. Failing this, try the citronella-spray collar, which is designed to squirt a lemon-scented spray at his nose every time he barks. Be sure to follow the instructions very carefully.

How can I stop him escaping from the garden?

There are two issues: hormones and confinement. If a female dog is in season, she is likely to try to escape to spend time with her suitors, while a male dog will travel many miles to sit waiting on her doorstep. Spaying and neutering are the obvious answers to the hormonal issue.

Some male (and female) dogs escape from the garden for no reason other than a sense of adventure. So if your dog is a bit of a tramp, you need give him plenty of stimulation and exercise him for half an hour twice daily. A bored dog will get up to mischief.

How can we make sure he has a good time when we're away?

Dogs enjoy holidays too! If you cannot take yours with you on yours, then let him have his own. There are plenty of great boarding kennels around and your dog can be pampered, hang out with the other dogs, be taken on walks, have one to one playtimes and all sorts of extras that won't cost an arm and a leg. Follow personal recommendations, then go and check the kennels out for yourself.

Look out for a high staff to dog ratio; is it friendly and clean; and do the dogs staying there at the time of your visit look happy and lively or sad and unkempt? Then, the only thing that need concern you when you return will be whether Pooch will want to go back to your boring old routine after having had such a good time at dog camp!

Dog Day Afternoon...
TV matinees for mutts?

Did you know that dogs see television much more clearly in the UK than in the USA? The more lines the TV signal is transmitted at, the clearer the picture for dogs. With High Definition on the way, soon even more dogs will be joining in the pastime! This can, of course, be useful because some broadcasts can have a calming effect and hold your dog's attention while you get on with other things. You can even get your dog a video/DVD designed especially for dogs to watch and entertain them. These are easy to search out online. Just try not to let TV take over his life and slide into the introduction of TV meals! You could, of course, switch off the goggle box and get back to the good old days of taking your dog out for a walk and a game of fetch.

CHAPTER 6

sick as a dog?

Should I introduce him to puppy love?

This is an area where it is wrong to put human thoughts and feelings into the minds of dogs. A male dog will have a strong urge to link up with a female dog when she is on heat, but when the scent of the female has gone, so has his physical urge. Dogs live in the moment and are unable to reflect on romantic matters. However, they are social animals and generally enjoy the company of other dogs. So, yes, it is a good idea to find a friend (girl or boy) for him. But if it's a girl, make sure both of them are neutered first.

How can I make him be more pleasant to his doctor?

OK, so your dog doesn't like going to the vet. Now let's try and view this from his perspective for a moment. You drag him along to a place he rarely goes, he is forced to wait surrounded by all kinds of other animals, all equally bemused and nervous …some sick.

Then he's called in to see a stranger who places him on a table. (Hang on…I'm not allowed on the table at home.) Then the stranger pokes him, inserts instruments into all kinds of orifices, and then he gets a needle stuck in his neck.

It is a scary and unusual routine for a dog to go through. So the thing is to make it a better known and more pleasant experience for him. Drop by the vet from time to time if only to pick up some worming tablets or to get weighed so it is not all about 'the table'. Soon he and the staff will get to know each other and the place will take on a less threatening aspect, making it easier for everyone to relax…except about that place where the thermometer goes!

Walking when he hasn't had his puppy shots. Is it worth the risk?

We all want to show off our new puppy, but listen up: vaccinations protect puppies against a range of serious, potentially fatal infections, including parvovirus, distemper, infectious hepatitis and Leptospirosis. If a pup is exposed to one of these infectious organisms before he has completed his vaccine course, there is a significant risk that he will develop the illness. Ask your own vet when the vaccine protection will become fully protective. It's usually 7 to 14 days after the final injection, and from that point the world is his oyster.

Should I stop my dog licking my face?

Some people say that a dog licking a human is a submissive gesture, and that there is no harm in it. It has also been said that dogs carry fewer harmful bacteria in their mouths than humans, and that therefore the risk of infections being passed on may not be high. My view would be that an occasional accidental lick might not do any harm, but it doesn't seem sensible to make a habit of it, in either direction.

Dogs are scavengers by nature and pick up all sorts of foul-looking objects in their mouths when they are out and about. They are also avid cleaners of every part of their own bodies. I haven't yet seen a detailed analysis of the bacterial load on a dog's tongue, but I don't need to: it's common sense that some things are yucky, and having your face and lips licked by a dog is one of them.

How often should his bedding be changed?

It is said, 'Let sleeping dogs lie', but just where and what on is down to you. Most dogs, like teenagers, are happy to have their bedding cleaned by putting it through the washing machine no more than once a month. If, after this is done, the bed still has a nose-shrivelling pong, it may be linked to a bacterial or yeast infection of the dog's coat. You can control this with a twice-weekly washing of the dog using a special shampoo. So sniff around. If your dog's bedding and coat seem fustier than usual, pop him along to the vet; otherwise look forward to twelve straightforward dog–bed washdays per year.

Doggy breath?

Hey dog breath! There are three possible cause of halitosis in dogs:

1. Dental. Have a look at his teeth and gums. If you can see thick brown tartar on the teeth, and swollen, reddened gums, he needs to visit the vet for a dental clean up.

2. Skin disease around the mouth. It can affect the folds of skin around the lower lips. You need to take him to the vet.

3. The digestive system. Foul-smelling gases are often produced while food is digested, and this often drifts up into the breath. If this is the cause, you should try a new type of diet.

To insure or not to insure?

Dogs can be clumsy and accident prone. They swallow objects that they shouldn't and chase cars, to name two of their hazardous activities. The resulting veterinary treatment can be eye-wateringly expensive. Invest in some pet insurance and peace of mind that if your pet subsequently has an accident or develops an illness, you will then be able to make decisions based entirely on what is best for him, rather than having to carry out an economic analysis of whether or not you can afford the procedure. There are many different policies out there, and you need to read the fine print carefully before signing up.

He always refuses to take his tablets. Any tips?

In both the animal and the human world some medications taste foul! There's no getting away from it. Thankfully there are some preparations for dogs that can be applied through the skin between the shoulder blades, but sooner or later something is going to crop up that requires him swallowing a tablet. This is why the hotdog was invented! Next time you have to administer a tablet, chop a cooked hotdog into several small pieces and secrete the tablet in one of them. Praise your dog and feed him two or three pieces in fairly rapid succession and then the piece containing the pill, letting him see you ready with another piece to follow it. Chances are he will gulp it down without even noticing.

Will my dog forgive me for having him neutered?

Dogs can survive without being neutered, but for the average household pet, it is the best decision. Neutering makes a dog's life simpler, and most dogs are better, healthier pets for it.

Mammary cancer, the most common cancer to affect female dogs, is prevented almost completely if they are spayed before their first season, and there are a number of illnesses affecting male dogs, including prostate problems and hernias, that virtually never occur in castrated animals. They can't thank you for sparing them from these, but then the concepts of blame, anger and forgiveness don't exist either in the bow-wow-now world of a dog. In short, they simply don't understand they are being neutered.

Talk about the subject in more detail with your vet, but it makes no sense to put your human thoughts into your dog's head.

Author biography

Peter Wedderburn is a vet in a 'companion animal' practice working only with pets. He writes a weekly column in the *Daily Telegraph* and the *Evening Irish Herald* and appears regularly as 'Pete the Vet' on Ireland's TV3. He lives in County Wicklow, Ireland, with his wife and two daughters and a menagerie of animals and birds.